MANGER

Poems selected by
LEE BENNETT HOPKINS

Illustrations by
HELEN CANN

EERDMANS BOOKS FOR YOUNG READERS

GRAND RAPIDS, MICHIGAN • CAMBRIDGE, U.K.

For Mary Fischer . . .
whom
I
herald.
— *L. B. H.*

To Molly and Daisy Cann with
much love, Auntie Helen, x.
— *H. C.*

ACKNOWLEDGMENTS

Thanks are due to Curtis Brown, Ltd., for use of "Old Owl": copyright © 2014 by Rebecca Kai Dotlich;
"Fish": copyright © 2014 by Lee Bennett Hopkins; "Horse": copyright © 1992 by X. J. Kennedy, first appeared in
The Beasts of Bethlehem, published by Margaret K. McElderry Books; "Wren": copyright © 2014 by Prince Redcloud;
"Sheep's Whisper": copyright © 2014 by Amy Ludwig VanDerwater; "Dog at the Stable":
copyright © 1990 by Jane Yolen. All used by permission of Curtis Brown, Ltd.

Thanks are also due for commissioned works used by permission of the respective poets, who control all rights:
Alma Flor Ada for "Llama"; Joan Bransfield Graham for "Rooster"; Michele Krueger for "Spider's Gift";
Jude Mandell for "Curious Cat"; Marilyn Nelson for "Mousesong";
Ann Whitford Paul for "Cow"; Alice Schertle for "Littlest Goat."

Illustrations © 2014 Helen Cann

Published in 2014 by Eerdmans Books for Young Readers,
an imprint of Wm. B. Eerdmans Publishing Co.
2140 Oak Industrial Dr. NE
Grand Rapids, Michigan 49505
P.O. Box 163, Cambridge CB3 9PU U.K.

www.eerdmans.com/youngreaders

Manufactured at Tien Wah Press
in Malaysia in February 2014, first printing
20 19 18 17 16 15 14   9 8 7 6 5 4 3 2 1

Library of Congress Cataloging-in-Publication Data

Manger / edited by Lee Bennett Hopkins ; illustrated by Helen Cann.
pages cm
ISBN 978-0-8028-5419-3
1. Christian poetry, American. 2. Children's poetry, American. 3. Jesus Christ — Nativity — Juvenile poetry. 4. Crèches (Nativity scenes) — Juvenile poetry.
I. Hopkins, Lee Bennett, editor of compilation. II. Cann, Helen, 1969- illustrator.
PS595.C47M36 2014
811.008'03823 — dc23
2013044516

The illustrations were created with watercolor, collage, and mixed media.
The display type was set in Amerigo BT.
The text type was set in Gil Sans.

CONTENTS

Introduction

Christmas Eve.

Midnight.

God grants
all creatures
big and small
the power
of human thought
or speech
to welcome
and comfort
Baby Jesus
lying in a
manger.

Here are their
responses to
God's gift.

Lee Bennett Hopkins

5

Rooster

Though it's not
          dawn,
and stars still
          blaze,
I, who announce
          the start
          of days,

feel the need
          to crow
          to herald

a tiny prince
who'll change
          the world.

Joan Bransfield Graham

Sheep's Whisper

Suddenly I speak.
I don't know what to say.
We've never had a child here
snuggled in our hay.

I've never seen a baby
or so much golden light.
I lean toward him.

I whisper
through
this sacred moonlit night —

"They say you are the shepherd.
Small one, is it true?

Look!

One star is
winking,
        blinking,
                twinkling
just
for
you."

Amy Ludwig VanDerwater

8

9

Horse

On Christmas Eve, the night unique,
they say we beasts find tongues to speak.

Yet at this crib I am so stirred
that, staring, I can say no word.

X. J. Kennedy

Curious Cat

Whiskers twitching in suspense,
fur puffed,
ruffled,
muscles tensed,

I tiptoe near,
gaze down to see
a babe —
whose sweet arms
welcome me.

I am but Cat,
a creature wild.

What gifts have I
to give
this Child?

No gold,
no frankincense,
no myrrh,
only my quiet
soothing purr.

Jude Mandell

12

Mousesong

Something called me out my hiding place
to creep through a forest of human legs.

Something brought me to crouch here, visible.

Something made me stand up on my hind feet
to see how the white light from that big star
mixes with gold light from the manger
I've scrounged under every day of my life.

"Welcome, Baby King of the Universe —
by your light I see a lifetime of seeds!"

Marilyn Nelson

Dog at the Stable

I was quiet, as the father bade me,
and I barked at no one who came.
I kept my head between my paws
until She called my name.

But then I stood to shake myself
and, silent, viewed the Child.
Who would have thought a Master might
remain so meek, so mild?

Jane Yolen

Cow

No wonder you cry,
little one,
a bright star lights
the night, and you lie
in a bed of hay
that's not soft,
or smooth.

Close your eyes,
little one,
I have a way
to soothe you.
Listen well
to my lullaby
of moo.

Ann Whitford Paul

Wren

"Before you whimper
again,"
said wren,

"I'll shed
a few feathers
to put in your bed,

softly
placed
under
your tiny
blessed
head."

Prince Redcloud

21

Old Owl

I am
Grandfather Owl,
Keeper of skies.

What gift can I give Him?

My
    secret
        of
            wise.

Rebecca Kai Dotlich

Fish

Despite
the world's
sudden glee

we cannot leave
our home — the sea

but
we will
swish and flap
each fin

for
we, too,

welcome
Jesus
in.

Lee Bennett Hopkins

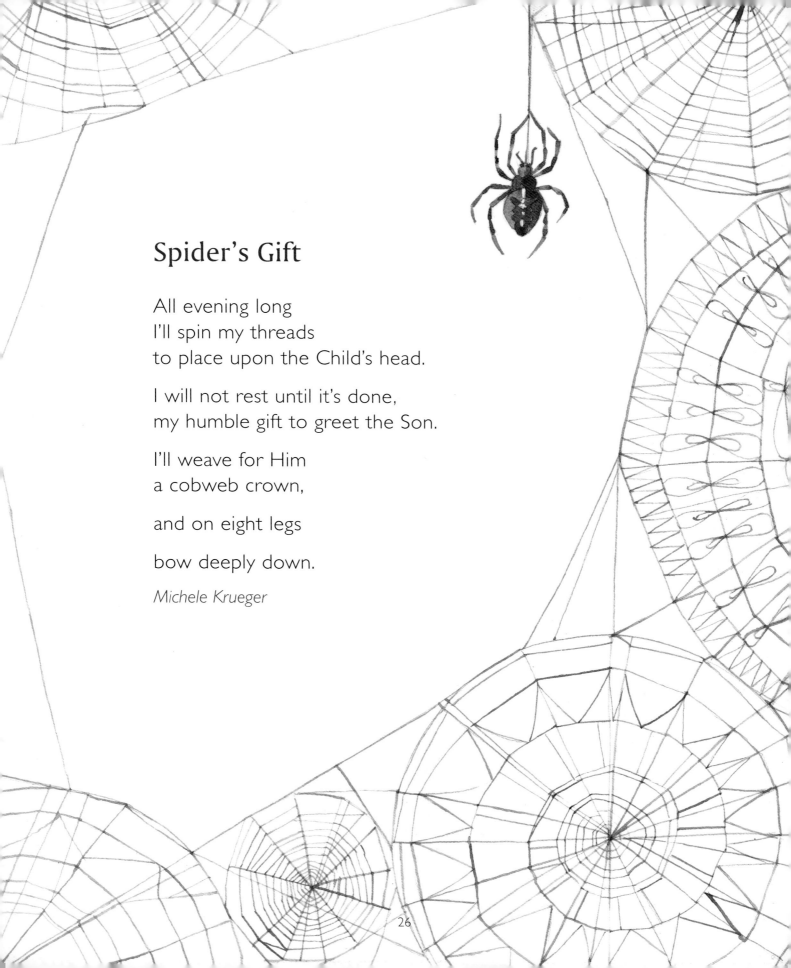

Spider's Gift

All evening long
I'll spin my threads
to place upon the Child's head.

I will not rest until it's done,
my humble gift to greet the Son.

I'll weave for Him
a cobweb crown,

and on eight legs

bow deeply down.

Michele Krueger

Llama

You are so small
sweet baby
upon the straw.

I so tall
stare at you
and softly whisper,

"May my wool
be woven
into soft blankets

to keep you
forever warm."

Alma Flor Ada

28

Littlest Goat

Donkey pushed in front of me.
I couldn't see at all.
Bossy Sheep said, "Go outside!
No jumping in the stall!"

But Mary smiled and Joseph rubbed
my muzzle with his staff
when I jumped over Donkey's back
and made the baby laugh.

Alice Schertle

from

The Friendly Beasts

"I," said the donkey,
shaggy and brown,

"I carried His mother
up hill and down;

I carried her safely
to Bethlehem town.''

"I,'' said the donkey,
shaggy and brown.

Traditional

33